My Couplet Runneth Over

The World Now & Then

(in rhyming 2-liners)

Barbara P. Alpren

ISBN:1470127555
978-1-4701-2755-8

For my loving son, Tom.
In the history of mankind,
no one had a son like him.

~ CONTENTS ~

~ HISTORY ~

The Spanish Inquisition
In fourteen hundred ninety two
It wasn't good to be a Jew.

~

Abraham Lincoln
Emancipation brought him fame,
And now a tunnel bears his name.

~

Attila the Hun
I once had a date with Attila the Hun.
He pillaged and ravaged and gosh it was fun!

The Thirty Years War and the Hundred Years War

One was short and one was long -

Either way they both were wrong.

~

The Story of Egypt

Cleopatra, they say, had the world in her grasp,

But she died very young 'cause she had a big asp.

~

The Roman Empire

When Caesar crossed the Rubicon

His mother wondered where he'd gone.

~

The Explorers

Columbus, who came on the Santa Maria,

Gave most of the natives some free gonorrhea.

Joan of Arc

When she tried to save France she was only 14,

She was burned at the stake, which I think was quite mean.

~

Julius Caesar

Friends, Romans and countrymen, lend me your ears.

My toga, forsooth, is a schmatte from Sears.

~

The End of the Dinosaurs

What killed off all the dinosaurs? What caused their sorry fate?

The creatures were so hideous, they couldn't find a date!

~

King John at Runnymede

He signed the Magna Carta, insuring civil rights.

He wore the royal raiment – he looked so good in tights.

Nurse Florence Nightingale

She went to Crimea and hasn't been found.

(Whenever you need them, they're never around!)

~

You Dirty Rat

Quite long ago (the date is vague),

Some Europeans spread the plague.

~

Henry the Eighth

The marrying kind, he had multiple mates:

One Jane and two Ann's and a trio of Kates.

~

The First Thanksgiving

The pilgrims sailed to Plymouth Rock to find religious freedom.

The Injuns found the starving flock and felt obliged to feed 'em.

The Shtetl

The yenta complained when the Cossacks had come:

"So what can you do? A pogrom's a pogrom!"

⁓

Sacagawea, Indian Guide

Young Lewis and Clark misbehaved in the dark with beautiful Sacagawea.

She knew what they meant when they entered her tent and told them to

shove the idea.

⁓

The Bloody Napoleonic Wars

"Waterloo, Schmorterloo," Bonaparte said.

"My hemorrhoids are bleeding, I'm going to bed."

⁓

Lizzie Borden

Lizzie Borden was a tad

Impolite to Mom and Dad.

Ronald Reagan

Smiling liar, hogged the scenes,

Gave the nation jelly beans.

~

Nancy Reagan, Lady in Red

Fashionista, heart of lead,

Ergo: both her children fled.

~

Laura Bush

Little Texas country mouse,

Much, much nicer than her spouse.

~ TODAY ~

The Children's Crusade
Kindergartners, if you fail,
You will not get in to Yale.

~

The Bible
The Bible must be selling well —
It's in your room in your motel.

~

The Immaculate Conception
Barren couples have one wish:
Romance in a Petri dish.

30 Something

My grandchild got her Ph.D., that's lovely but I guess

She'd swap it in a minute for a simple MRS.

~

Big Screen T.V.

I saw the new Sony —Good God it has grown!

It comes with a zip code completely its own!

~

Tiger Woods

Tiger Woods, with his stable of sluts,

Showed them all his extra long putz!

~

Pest Control

To fix those telemarketers, wherever they may roam,

My automatic answer is, "My missy, she no home."

Sardines

On planes they removed all the seats in the place,

When people are standing they take up less space.

~

Stick Figures

The models on the runway look so famished and so thin,

Your instinct when you see them is to call their next of kin!

~

Vending Machines

Machines are selling everything: lasagna by the portion,

A living will, a tuna wrap, a fairly clean abortion.

~

Who's that Walking Down the Street?

I wish I wore a burka in a country with a shah,

I wouldn't need a girdle or a hairdo or a bra!

Naming the Baby

The chances are my pregnant friend is carrying a Chloe,

A Madison, a Tiffany, a Zachary or Zoey.

~

Queen Elizabeth II

She never smiles or eats a sub,

She wears her handbag in the tub.

~

The Amazing New Smart Phone

This do-it-all gadget can paint your garage,

Can treat you for shingles and do decoupage.

~

Pax Vobiscum

For global peace I have a plan -

Ignore the states that end with "stan."

Gotcha!

Pleasant thought that warms me well:

OJ's rotting in a cell!

~

Man's Best Friend

My doggie looks a lot like me observers often say,

So now I'm getting Botox 'cause my dog is pure Shar-Pei.

~

Yankee, Go Home

The more we try and try to please,

The more they hate us over seas.

~

Duchess of York (Fergie)

Unfrocked Royal British tramp,

Won't be pictured on a stamp.

Nancy Pelosi

The speaker has a nasty smirk.

I wish she'd look for other work.

~

A Nazi and Sarah Palin at Sea

There's room for just one in the lifeboat,

the captain explained to the crew,

I have to choose one or the other, I'm holding my nose when I do.

~ ARTS & SCIENCES ~

The Pinter of Our Discontent
Damn it, Harold, help us out,
Tell us what your play's about!

~

A Sore Thumb
An architect conceived a crime
And christened it the Guggenheim.

~

The Theatre
I tried to date the great John Gielgud,
But he said he didn't feel good.

The Toast of Paris

The famous philosopher, Sartre,

Was famous because he was smartre.

~

Thomas Chippendale

If Chippendale had signed your chairs,

You'd have some very wealthy heirs.

~

Pop Culture

I like music with melody, plays with a plot,

These basic essentials pop-artists ain't got.

~

Albert Einstein

Einstein, with his brain so rare,

Never learned to comb his hair.

Evolution

According to Darwin it's plain as can be:

My grandmother's uncle was born in a tree.

～

Because of Thomas Edison

Menlo Park

Isn't dark!

~ ECONOMY ~

The Recession

To market, to market, to buy a fine roast.

Home again, home again, tuna on toast.

~

Bum Steer

No matter how much dough you make,

You can't afford a Kobe steak.

~

Broadway, 1933

Dinner at the steakhouse, theatre tickets too,

Set you back ten dollars, that's for both of you!

The BMW

Though the price is high on the BMW,

It's a damn good buy, so it shouldn't trouble you.

~

Wall Street

I'm losing money everyday, my stocks are down and dismal.

The market's driving me to drink – a drink of Pepto Bismol!

~

Property Taxes

They raise my taxes every year...I helplessly protest it.

I hung a birdhouse on a tree...Ye gods! They just assessed it!

~

High Interest Credit Cards

Once a month I pay off loans,

It's lots of fun, like kidney stones.

Happy Motoring

My shiny new car is expensive and nifty,

It cost what my house did in late 1950.

~ POET'S CORNER ~

I think that I shall never see
A really good domestic brie.

~

Once upon a midnight dreary
I got mugged in downtown Erie.

~

My heart leaps up when I behold,
My gorgeous friend is looking old.

The boy stood on the burning deck —
I hope insurance sent a check.

~

In Flander's Field where pollen grows,
I wipe my eyes, un-snot my nose.

~

O wad some Power the giftie gie us
To see ourselves aboard a Prius!

~

I wandered lonely as a cloud
Because there ain't no sex allowed.

~

I shot an arrow in the air -----
Too bad the Goodyear blimp was there.

~ CHILD'S GARDEN OF REVERSES ~

Mary had a little lamb,
She also had some veal.

~

Simple Simon
Broke her hymen.

~

Rock-a-bye baby in the treetop,
Get the kid down or I'm calling a cop.

Mary, Mary quite contrary,

Did you know your legs were hairy?

~

There was a little girl

Who looked like Milton Berle.

~

Little Bo Peep has lost her sheep,

So next year's sweaters won't be cheap.

~

There was a crooked man who walked a crooked mile,

And now that he's the mayor, he'll make a crooked pile.

~

Little Jack Horner

Peed in the corner.

Humpty Dumpty sat on a wall,
Was laid by a chick in a comfortable stall.

~

Now I lay me down to sleep,
I count the flock that screwed Bo Peep.

~

Hansel and Gretl
Ain't from the Shtetl.

~

Diddle, diddle dumpling, my son John,
Daddy went a-humping, now he's gone.

~ LANGUAGE ~

Three Little Words

The letter "P" is tricky for its has a Grecian stem.
It's hiding out in ptarmigan, psoriasis and phlegm.

~

Try to Speak Good!

Mistakes in English grammar now have reached an all-time high,
Like "different than" or "laying down" or "helping Bob and I."

~

A Spoonerism

I never liked my neighbor Charley,
And often tell him: "Chuck you, Farley."

Proper English

Use consensus <u>or</u> opinion, they're redundant, take your choice,

They are in the same dominion as the Bentley or Rolls Royce.

⁓

Look Alikes

Alpacas seem a lot like llamas,

Like semicolons are to commas.

⁓

We Win

For enemy losses we've smugly enjoyed,

The Germans invented the term schadenfreude.

⁓

Interior Design

"Amusing" and "clever" are words I abhor,

Describing a trendy, self-conscious decor.

The Pen of My Uncle

I've studied French but, mon ami, my aptitude is truant,
Yet tiny tots in gay Paree are maddeningly fluent.

~

The Trojan Horse

If someone tries to sell you a massive horse of wood,
Do offer this suggestion: Kind sir, hub dir in buhd!

~ RELIGION ~

Organized Religion

"Love thy neighbor," Bibles tell.

"Worship <u>my</u> way, or in hell!"

~

Cardinal Sin

Priests led more unblemished lives

Long ago when they had wives.

~

What's in a Name?

With a name like "Smuckers," it has to be good.

With a name like "Lipschitz," I'd swap if I could.

New Year's at the Vatican

The Pope told the Rabbi, "Let's heal the divide."

"Good Yontif, my Pontiff!" the Rabbi replied.

~

Man of Letters

My temple has a scholarly chaplain,

His moniker is Phi Beta Kaplan.

~

Mystery Man

His name isn't Patrick, he has no tattoo,

He doesn't eat headcheese...you guessed, he's a Jew!

~

Peaceable Kingdom

Imperfect human beings need to read these words once more:

The fish don't build cathedrals, but they don't engage in war.

The Miracle Worker

Say a prayer at the shrine of St. Anne de Beaupré---

In a minute, voilà, throw your crutches away.

～

Native Americans

If I had Choctaw in my genes,

My wigwam could have slot machines.

～

Well-bred

It's good to be Jewish, I'm telling you why:

The bagel, the challah, the great seeded rye.

～

The Reformation

Martin Luther, German monk,

Thought that Roman Catholics stunk!

Celebration

From the Dardanelles to the Panama Isthmus,

You can hear the bells of a Goyisha Christmas.

~ HEALTH ~

Elizabeth Arden

The beauty-purveyor, Elizabeth Arden,

Helps women look young while their arteries harden.

~

Bad Habits

Smoking is a habit that can rush you to your coffin,

Quitting isn't hard to do.... I've done it very often.

~

Brush Up

A talent that I wish I'd lack,

Is building uninvited plaque.

The Proctologist

The greetings are brief when I see my physician:

Hello, drop your pants and assume the position.

~

On the Pill

Though once you had to have a shrink at every costly session,

Today you take a simple pill and treat your own depression.

~

The Check-Up

Doctor's orders, feared and cruel:

"Bring a sample of your stool."

~

"Misery"

I'm sick with the flu and the feverish spurts.

Except for my eyelashes, everything hurts.

When My Ox is Not Being Gored

I don't complain about their pain when friends are feeling sickly,

And other people's pregnancies (to me) go very quickly.

~ FOOD & DIET ~

Food, Glorious Food
My butt, despite the diet soda,
Is twice the size of South Dakota!

~

Yum!
Man invented quiche and brandy —
<u>God</u> created chocolate candy!

~

Intestinal Fortitude
Eating junk food is, no doubt,
Garbage in and garbage out.

Jennie Craig Dropout

Models with your size 2 butts,

Other women hate your guts!

~

Ditch the Diet Books

Diet that's a cinch to follow:

Eat a lot but just don't swallow.

~

The Wages of Sin

Hot fudge sundae Monday night,

Tuesday will be cellulite.

~

The Jaguar

Those sporty cars are not for me, they're low and I'm too heavy,

My husband drives an XKE.... I follow in the Chevy!

Sweet Mystery of Life

A day without friction's a day for thanksgiving,

A day without chocolate's a day not worth living.

~

Fresh Fruit

The doctor said, "Eat lots of fruit to keep your body fit."

I'm following his orders with this nice banana split!

~

The Big Cheese

Too much Parmesan and Gouda

You will have a shape like Buddha!

~

Good Taste

I never trust a chef who's thin,

Expect, at least, a double chin!

Diabetes and a Touch of Heart Failure

I'm allowed the hot pastrami and the double chocolate malt,

Just as long as I can find them minus sugar, fat and salt.

~

Voices

I have brownies in the freezer and they call my name at night,

They're like evil chocolate sirens and they sing until I bite!

~

Que Será

Life is uncertain and can't be rehearsed,

Life is uncertain, so eat dessert first.

~

For My Enemy

Excellent nutrition guide:

Only eat it if it's fried.

Plus Size

To curb my overeating mood

I picture Buddy Hackett nude.

~

Me and the British Empire

Concerning eats: I live on sweets, on mounds of curly fries,

The sun regrets it never sets on my wondrous thunder thighs!

~

The Nose Knows

I like the smell of French Chanel, but when I first awaken,

I'd rather sniff a little whiff of noisy frying bacon.

~

Dry Martinis

After having one martini, I'm not funny, I admit,

After two or three, however, I'm a devastating wit!

Rx

When happiness is on the wane

I phone for take-out pork lo mein.

~

Big

I used to gorge on meals I cooked, my biscuits drove me daft,

Till someone said he thought I looked like William Howard Taft.

~ AGING:
THE POST MENOPAUSE PAGES ~

Lest We Forget

My memory is still quite sharp, although I'm 87.

My aging son belongs to AARP–I think his name is Kevin!

~

60th Wedding Anniversary

When we're in bed each night at nine,

His teeth are soaking next to mine.

~

The Lord Giveth and the Lord Taketh

The hair that used to crown my head,

Is thriving on my chin instead!

The Nursing Home

At Shady Pines when we play dots,

We just connect our liver spots.

~

Victoria's Secret

My fashion savvy never ends—

My lingerie is by Depends.

~

My Granddaughter

I'm feeling old, perhaps because

My grandchild started menopause.

~

Hair

Guys go bald and dolls get hairy,

Follicles make aging scary.

A Senior Moment

My feet were up in stirrups with the doctor underneath,

'Twas then that I remembered I forgot to wear my teeth!

~

Ninety Candles on My Cake

I used to love to lunch with friends, but as I look ahead,

I'll do my lunching all alone, 'cause all my friends are dead.

~

Silver Threads Among the Gold

My dear, when middle age begins,

Relax and take it on your chins.

~

On Being Ninety

It's such a long adventure on my trip from womb to tomb,

No matter where I venture, I'm the oldest in the room.

My Dentures I

My gums are old, my teeth are new.

Inside my mouth I'm 22.

~

My Dentures II

My gums are old, my teeth are new.

I'll gladly chew your meat for you.

~

Merry Widow

I've been a widow many years, I miss the sound of snoring,

I lay me down to sleep alone...no runs, no hits, no scoring.

~

Antique: At least 100 Years Old

Be gentle with collectibles, like Wedgwood or Belleek,

And careful how you handle *me*, I'm almost an antique!

My New Hearing Aid

A feature that I just adore:

It tunes you out if you're a bore.

~

Depression

Some women after childbirth suffer sadness and distress,

I'm 60 years post-partum and *Marone*, I'm still a mess!

~

Lucky Me

The best things God bestowed on me

Are Medicare and Sara Lee.

~

Through the Looking Glass

If you're wrinkled, old and ugly and your hair is thin and grey,

Keep away from every mirror, you'll feel better right away.

Take a Breather

I've tried to look fetching with make-up and clothes,

But how can I do it with tubes up my nose?

~

No News is Good News

I know I'm still living by using my wits:

I read all the papers and check the obits.

~

My Grandchildren

My grandkids are athletic and they love the great outdoors,

They're also smart and gifted and much prettier than yours!

~

My Children's Children

My grandkids come on weekends and they fill up all my beds,

On Sunday night I'm glad to see the backs of all their heads.

~ POTPOURI ~

Delicious

What's twice as nice as being rich?

The heaven when you scratch an itch.

~

Circus Side Show

Siamese Twins have to share vital parts:

One wets his pants while the other one farts!

~

Pollyanna

If your face is plagued with pimples,

View them as inverted dimples.

Paris, France

The Saint-Honoré is like Madison Avenue,

With famous boutiques which you've heard of, or havenue?

⁓

Dred Scot

A lecherous laddie was wearing a kilt,

And nothing beneath it to cover his guilt!

⁓

Duh

Concerning stupid people, the Lord must really love them,

And that must be the reason he made so many of them!

⁓

Natural Gas on a Bus

Eat beans and look innocent there in the aisle,

And while you're performing continue to smile.

Happy Talk

My life is almost perfect, just a smidgen less than great,

And that is why I'm saying that I'm sitting on cloud eight.

~

Planned Parenthood

If men bore the babies, if men were restyled,

Those cowards would <u>never</u> have more than one child!

~

Chacum a Son Gout

Some people tango and some people knit,

I, to be honest, do nothing but sit.

~

Safe

My diamonds are flawless, with hardly a fault,

They glitter and sparkle and dress up my vault.

Short Story

"I'm suing the city," cried dumpy Miss Cass.

"For building the sidewalk too close to my ass!"

~

Bargains

The coupons in the Sunday news

Are not for stuff that I can use.

~

Old Time T.V.

The pretty young ladies of Petticoat Junction

Were seldom concerned with erectile dysfunction.

~

Lent

For Lent I'd like to give up things, unhappily among us:

Like income tax, anchovy paste, Republicans and fungus.

Dollar Diplomacy

I never was a pretty girl, a charmer or a cutie,

But when my papa struck it rich, they found my inner beauty.

~

Pollyanna Lives

If your basement's fully flooded after days and weeks of raining, Now

your property is "waterfront," so quit your damn complaining.

~

Hershey, Pennsylvania

A sweet old town you must not miss, was built by a candy Czar.

It's where you'll blow a chocolate kiss, and drink at a Hershey bar.

NOT YET

Now that I'm 90, though I'm not too spry,

I'm still quite cheery as my time grown nigh.

You can't live forever, but I sure will try!

ABOUT THE AUTHOR

Barbara Parsonnet Alpren is a 92-year-old humorist whose poems and limericks have been published in the *New York Times* and *New York Magazine*. She is the author of numerous musical parodies for community theaters and declined the invitation to write the lyrics for a hit Broadway show because she was "too busy." Her education at Parsons School of Design led her into successful careers as a fashion illustrator at Bergdorf Goodman, sculptor, interior designer and antique dealer. She lives in West Orange, New Jersey.

Made in the USA
Charleston, SC
09 July 2012